Simple Explanation

Of

Artificial intelligence

Dear readers,

Welcome to the book "Simple Explanation of Artificial Intelligence."

Artificial intelligence has taken on a significant role in our world today and influences our daily lives in many ways. In this book, we aim to provide you with the basics of artificial intelligence without getting lost in technical details.

Our goal is to offer you simple and understandable explanations so that you can grasp the fundamental principles of artificial intelligence. We will cover various topics such as machine learning, neural networks, and computer vision. Additionally, we will address ethical questions that arise from the use and development of artificial intelligence.

We want to give you an understanding of how artificial intelligence impacts our world and how it could evolve in the future. The book is designed to be informative yet exciting to read, sparking your curiosity.

A heartfelt thank you to everyone who contributed to the creation of this book and to you, dear readers, for your interest in the fascinating world of artificial intelligence.

Enjoy reading and exploring artificial intelligence!

Warm regards,

Kevin van Olafson

Chapter 1: Introduction to Artificial Intelligence

Welcome to the fascinating world of Artificial Intelligence! In this chapter, we'll delve into the basics and gain a comprehensive insight into this exciting topic.

Artificial Intelligence, also known as AI, is a field of computer science that deals with the development of systems exhibiting human-like intelligence. The goal of AI is to empower computers to learn, understand, think, and act intelligently - much like we humans do.

However, the idea of Artificial Intelligence is not new. As early as the 1950s, scientists began developing computers that aimed to simulate human thought processes. At that time, technology was limited, and it took some time for AI to become what it is today.

Over the decades, AI has continuously evolved and now influences many aspects of our daily lives. From voice recognition systems like Siri or Google Assistant to personalized recommendations in streaming services and even self-driving cars - Artificial Intelligence is already present in numerous fields and impacts our lives in various ways.

The applications of Artificial Intelligence are virtually limitless. It can aid in analyzing complex problems, recognizing patterns, making decisions, and even fulfilling creative tasks. From medicine and finance to manufacturing - AI finds applications in a wide range of industries and offers great potential for efficiency improvement and solving complex challenges.

To better understand Artificial Intelligence, it's important to look at the different types of AI. Typically, we distinguish between weak AI and strong AI. Weak AI is specialized in specific tasks or problem domains, while strong AI possesses comprehensive human-like intelligence. However, strong AI is still in the developmental phase and poses a significant challenge.

Throughout this book, we will explore many exciting topics related to Artificial Intelligence. These include machine learning, neural networks, deep learning, natural language processing, computer vision, and many more aspects. You will discover that AI is a fascinating field that is constantly growing and profoundly shaping our future.

However, the development and application of Artificial Intelligence also raise challenges and ethical questions. It's important to consider topics such as responsibility, transparency, data privacy, and potential discrimination. In later chapters, we will delve deeply into these aspects and shed light on different perspectives.

Get ready to dive into the exciting world of Artificial Intelligence and explore its potentials. In the upcoming chapters, we will explore the history of Artificial Intelligence and see how it has evolved over time. Get ready for an exciting journey through the fascinating world of AI!

Chapter 2: The History of Artificial Intelligence

The history of Artificial Intelligence is a fascinating journey through decades of innovation, groundbreaking ideas, and continuous progress. In this chapter, we'll delve into the key milestones of AI history and understand how this captivating field has evolved over time.

The beginnings of Artificial Intelligence can be traced back to the 1950s when computers were still in their infancy, and technological capabilities were limited. It was during this time that the first concepts and ideas emerged on how to make machines develop human-like intelligence. One of the pioneers in this field was the mathematician and computer scientist Alan Turing, who already in 1950 developed the famous "Turing test" idea to determine whether a machine can exhibit intelligent behavior.

In the 1950s and 1960s, Artificial Intelligence experienced a surge driven by the emergence of new concepts and techniques. A significant milestone was the development of logic programming by John McCarthy, Marvin Minsky, and other scientists at Dartmouth College in 1956. This form of programming enabled computers to draw logical conclusions and solve complex problems.

Another milestone in the history of Artificial Intelligence was the development of expert systems in the 1960s and 1970s. These systems relied on extensive domain knowledge and rules to solve specific tasks or problems. A well-known example of an expert system is MYCIN, developed in the 1970s and used in medical diagnosis. Expert systems were groundbreaking as they demonstrated that computers are capable of making decisions based on specialized knowledge.

In the 1980s and 1990s, scientists began pursuing new approaches in AI research. An important development was the emergence of machine learning, where computers can learn from data and recognize patterns. This method enabled the training of AI systems and improved their performance. A significant milestone was the introduction of the backpropagation algorithm in the 1980s, which allowed for effective training of deep neural networks.

Another breakthrough in AI history was the rise of deep learning in the 2000s. This involves using deep neural networks to solve complex tasks. The increased availability of large datasets and improved computing power played a significant role in the development of deep learning. This technique achieved impressive advancements in areas such as image recognition, natural language processing, and robotics.

Today, we are in the midst of an AI revolution. Artificial Intelligence has made its way into our daily lives and influences numerous sectors such as communication, healthcare, transportation, finance, and entertainment. Self-driving cars, intelligent assistants, personalized recommendations, and automated processes are just a few examples of AI's impact on our modern society.

The history of Artificial Intelligence is marked by breakthroughs but also setbacks and controversial discussions. In the 1970s, for example, the disillusionment with the limited capabilities of AI systems led to a decline in interest and investments in the field, known as the "AI winter." However, AI research later continued, leading to new insights and successes.

The vision of strong AI surpassing human intelligence remains a challenge and subject of intense research. The development of Artificial General Intelligence (AGI) is still in its early stages and presents many technical and ethical challenges.

In the upcoming chapters, we will explore the fundamentals of machine learning, neural networks, deep learning, natural language processing, computer vision, and other important aspects of Artificial Intelligence. You will understand how these techniques work and the possibilities they offer. Additionally, we will address the ethical and societal implications of Artificial Intelligence to gain a comprehensive understanding of this fascinating field.

The history of Artificial Intelligence shows us that we are in a continuous process of innovation and advancement. It remains exciting to observe the groundbreaking developments that await us in the future and how Artificial Intelligence will continue to shape our world.

Chapter 3: Application of Artificial Intelligence

Artificial Intelligence (AI) has gained a lot of importance in recent years and has become an integral part of our modern society. In this chapter, we'll dive into the various uses of Artificial Intelligence and get a comprehensive overview of different areas where AI is applied.

Medicine and Healthcare:
AI has the potential to revolutionize medical diagnosis and treatment. From early disease detection to personalized medicine and surgical robotics, there are numerous applications that can improve the efficiency and accuracy of medical care.

Automotive Industry and Transportation:
Self-driving cars are a prime example of AI application in the transportation sector. By combining sensor data, machine learning, and advanced algorithms, autonomous vehicles can analyze traffic situations and safely navigate the roads.

Finance:
AI is increasingly used in the financial sector to detect fraud, assess risks, determine creditworthiness, and make automated trading decisions. Machine learning and neural networks enable the real-time analysis of large amounts of financial data and accurate predictions.

E-commerce and Personalized Recommendations:
Many online platforms use AI to generate personalized recommendations. Based on user behavior and preferences, algorithms can predict their interests and provide tailored suggestions, making the shopping process easier and increasing customer satisfaction.

Language Processing and Natural Language Understanding:
By employing AI technologies like speech recognition and chatbots, computers can understand and respond to natural language. These applications are found in virtual assistants like Siri, Alexa, or Google Assistant, as well as in customer support systems and translation programs.

Image Recognition and Computer Vision:
AI has made remarkable progress in image recognition and computer vision. From facial and object recognition to medical image analysis, these technologies enable the automatic evaluation of visual information and find applications in areas such as security, healthcare, and automation.

Environmental Protection and Sustainability:

AI can also make a significant contribution to environmental protection and sustainability. By analyzing large datasets, patterns can be identified to help address environmental issues like climate change, air pollution, and resource management.

Robotics and Automation:
AI technologies are increasingly used in robotics to develop autonomous robots that can work in various environments. From industrial applications to assisting and supporting people with disabilities, robots with AI capabilities can perform tasks more efficiently and safely.

Education:
Artificial Intelligence is increasingly entering the education sector. Through personalized learning, AI systems can analyze the learning progress of each student and offer individualized learning content and methods. Intelligent tutoring systems can assist students in solving tasks and expand their knowledge systematically.

Cybersecurity:
In an increasingly digitized world, cyberattacks pose a significant threat. Artificial Intelligence is used to detect attack patterns, identify intrusion attempts, and close security gaps. AI-powered systems can analyze large amounts of data to anticipate and defend against potential attacks.

Art and Creativity:
Artificial Intelligence has also made its way into the art field. From generating creative works like music and art to assisting filmmakers in post-production, AI offers new possibilities for artists and promotes collaboration between humans and machines.

Entertainment Industry:
The entertainment industry has recognized the potential of Artificial Intelligence and utilizes it for personalized recommendations of movies, music, and books. Furthermore, advanced animation techniques and virtual reality enable new immersive experiences for games and films.

Agriculture:
AI can be used in agriculture to optimize crop yields, detect plant diseases, improve irrigation, and reduce the use of pesticides. By combining sensor data, weather

forecasts, and machine learning, farmers can make informed decisions and implement more sustainable practices.

This list represents only a fraction of the application areas of Artificial Intelligence. The potential of AI is virtually limitless, and its impact will continue to shape our daily lives.

However, the application of Artificial Intelligence also poses ethical and societal challenges. Questions regarding privacy, accountability, bias, and job losses need to be carefully considered to ensure that AI is used for the benefit of humanity.

Chapter 4: Types of Artificial Intelligence

Artificial Intelligence (AI) is a fascinating and diverse field that encompasses various approaches and techniques. In this chapter, we will delve deeper into the different types of Artificial Intelligence and explore their functioning and application areas in more detail.

Weak Artificial Intelligence:
Weak AI, also known as Narrow AI, refers to systems that can solve specific tasks or problems they are designed for. This type of AI specializes in fulfilling a limited range of tasks at a high level. Examples of weak AI include voice recognition systems like Siri and Google Assistant, which can understand human language and respond accordingly. They can answer questions, process requests, and perform specific actions.

Strong Artificial Intelligence:
In contrast to weak AI, strong AI aims to achieve a general understanding and awareness similar to human thinking. Strong AI systems are intended to be capable of performing a variety of tasks and independently solving complex problems. However, this area of Artificial Intelligence is still in development and faces significant technical and ethical challenges. The idea of strong AI inspires many science fiction stories featuring intelligent robots or computers with human-like intelligence.

Machine Learning:
Machine Learning is a crucial approach within Artificial Intelligence. It refers to the ability of computers to learn from data and recognize patterns without being explicitly programmed. In machine learning, models are developed and trained by analyzing large amounts of data and identifying patterns or rules. These models can then be used to interpret future data or perform specific tasks. Machine learning is applied in various areas such as image recognition, natural language processing, fraud detection, and medical diagnosis.

Neural Networks:
Neural networks are another important approach in Artificial Intelligence, based on the principles of the human brain. These networks consist of interconnected artificial neurons that process and transmit information. By training the neural network, complex patterns in the data can be recognized, and tasks such as pattern recognition, language understanding, and decision-making can be executed. Neural networks have made significant progress in recent years and are widely used in many applications of Artificial Intelligence.

Genetic Algorithms:
Genetic algorithms are inspired by natural evolution and use principles like variation, selection, and mutation to find optimal solutions to complex problems. These algorithms are often employed in optimization, planning, and design. They enable exploring a large number of possible solutions and gradually generating the best solutions.

Expert Systems:
Expert systems aim to capture and reproduce the knowledge and skills of human experts in a specific domain. They utilize rules and logical reasoning to analyze problems and make informed decisions. Expert systems find applications in areas such as medical diagnosis, technical support, and legal advice.

Real-time AI:
Real-time AI refers to systems that can process data in real-time and make decisions. This type of AI is applied in areas such as autonomous driving, financial trading, and surveillance. Real-time AI allows analyzing complex information in real-time and generating quick responses or predictions.

<u>Robotic Artificial Intelligence</u>:
This type of AI combines Artificial Intelligence with robotics to develop autonomous robots capable of performing physical tasks in various environments. Robotic AI is applied in areas such as industrial manufacturing, logistics, healthcare, and even space exploration.

The different types of Artificial Intelligence offer various possibilities and potentials to solve complex problems and simulate human-like intelligence. Each type of Artificial Intelligence has its strengths and limitations, and the selection of the most suitable techniques depends on the specific task or application.

Through the continuous development and exploration of these types of Artificial Intelligence, we will be able to develop increasingly effective and versatile AI systems that can support and enrich us in many areas.

Chapter 5: Machine Learning

Machine learning is a fascinating field of artificial intelligence that allows computers to learn from data and perform tasks without being explicitly programmed. This discipline has made significant progress in recent years and has revolutionized numerous industries and application areas. In this chapter, we will delve into the fundamentals of machine learning and explore various techniques and approaches.

<u>Machine Learning</u>:
Before delving deeper into the techniques of machine learning, it's important to develop a basic understanding of what machine learning actually is. Essentially, it's an approach where computers develop and train models to learn from data and make predictions or perform tasks. The fundamental idea is to recognize patterns and relationships in the data to extract useful information.

<u>Supervised Learning</u>:
One of the most common techniques in machine learning is supervised learning. In this approach, the computer is provided with training data consisting of input-output pairs. The model is then trained to derive a function that maps the input to the

correct output. For example, a model could be trained based on historical data to make weather predictions. Supervised learning finds applications in various domains such as speech recognition, image understanding, and medical diagnosis.

Unsupervised Learning:
In contrast to supervised learning, unsupervised learning does not involve training with predetermined outputs. Instead, the model analyzes the data and automatically identifies patterns, structures, or relationships. It looks for natural groupings or patterns in the data to classify or segment them. Unsupervised learning is often used in areas such as customer analysis, data segmentation, and anomaly detection.

Reinforcement Learning:
Reinforcement learning refers to a type of learning where an agent interacts and learns by receiving environmental feedback. The goal is to learn an optimal action to fulfill a specific task. The model receives positive reinforcement for good actions and negative reinforcement for bad actions. Through repeated iterations, the model improves its skills and optimizes its decision-making. Reinforcement learning is often used in areas such as robotics, game strategies, and automated control.

Deep Learning:
Deep learning is a specialized type of machine learning that is based on artificial neural networks. These networks consist of layers of neurons that are interconnected and process information. Deep learning allows models to learn hierarchical representations and complex patterns in the data. This technique has made significant advancements in areas such as image and speech recognition, natural language processing, and autonomous driving.

Transfer Learning:
Transfer learning refers to the utilization of pre-trained models or knowledge to solve new tasks or problems. Instead of training a model from scratch, transfer learning can save time and resources. Existing models are applied to similar or related tasks and then adapted to the specific requirements. Transfer learning finds applications in many domains, especially when only limited training data is available.

Machine learning is an extremely versatile approach that enables computers to learn from experience and perform tasks in various domains. The diversity of techniques and approaches offers a wide range of possibilities to tackle complex problems and develop intelligent systems. With increasing availability of data and computing power, machine learning is expected to continue making groundbreaking advancements and influence our world in many ways.

"The chapter on 'Machine Learning' provides a comprehensive insight into this fascinating field of artificial intelligence. Machine learning allows computers to learn from data and perform tasks without being explicitly programmed. We have learned about various techniques and approaches in machine learning, including supervised learning, unsupervised learning, reinforcement learning, deep learning, and transfer learning."

Chapter 6: Neural Networks

In this chapter, we'll take a detailed look at neural networks. Neural networks are a fascinating part of machine learning that is based on the principle of artificially mimicking the human brain. They can recognize complex patterns in data and have applications in areas such as image recognition, speech understanding, text analysis, and much more.

A neural network consists of a collection of artificial neurons that are interconnected and process information. Each neuron takes input values, applies an activation function to those values, and passes an output value.
The connections between the neurons are represented by weights, which indicate the strength of the connection between neurons. By adjusting these weights during the training process, the network learns to interpret the input data correctly and recognize patterns.

The architecture of a neural network typically includes multiple layers of neurons. The first layer is called the input layer and takes in the input data. The last layer is called the output layer and produces the network's results. There can be one or more hidden layers in between.
The number of neurons in the layers and the connections between them are determined by the complexity of the task and the size of the dataset.

Training a neural network involves the iterative process of forward propagation and backward propagation of error. During forward propagation, the input data is passed through the network, taking into account the weights and activation functions of each neuron.

The network produces a prediction, which is compared to the actual output values. The difference between the prediction and the actual values is called the error.

Backward propagation is the crucial step in training a neural network. Here, the error is propagated backward through the network, and the weights are adjusted accordingly to minimize the error.

This process is facilitated by mathematical optimization algorithms like gradient descent. Through repeated training and adjustment of the weights, the network improves its ability to recognize patterns and make accurate predictions.

Neural networks have a wide range of applications and are used in various fields. In image recognition, they are used to identify objects, faces, or patterns in images. In the field of speech understanding, they enable speech recognition, language translation, and text analysis. They are also applied in medical diagnostics, financial analysis, customer behavior prediction, and many other areas.

Research and development of neural networks is an active field. New architectures, activation functions, and optimization algorithms are continuously explored to enhance the performance of the networks. Similarly, extensive work is being done to expand the application areas and employ artificial intelligence in more aspects of our lives.

The advancement of neural networks promises exciting possibilities for the future. With more powerful computers and larger datasets, we will be able to solve even more complex problems and make even more accurate predictions.

The progress in neural network technology will contribute to artificial intelligence being present in many aspects of our daily lives, helping us make better decisions and gain new insights.

However, the application of neural networks also poses challenges and ethical considerations. It is important to use artificial intelligence responsibly and ethically to minimize potential negative impacts.

Protecting privacy, avoiding discrimination, and ensuring transparency in decision-making processes are just some of the topics that need to be considered when applying neural networks.

Overall, neural networks are an exciting and promising field of artificial intelligence. They allow us to recognize complex patterns, make predictions, and solve problems in various domains. With further research and development, we will enhance the performance of neural networks and discover new applications. It's thrilling to see how this technology will evolve in the future and how it can positively impact our lives.

Chapter 7: Deep Learning

In this chapter, we'll dive deep into the world of deep learning. Deep learning is a special form of machine learning that relies on neural networks and is known for its ability to learn complex hierarchies of features in data. With the help of deep neural networks, deep learning enables profound analysis and processing of data, leading to remarkable advancements in various fields of artificial intelligence.

Deep learning models consist of multiple layers of neurons, referred to as deep neural networks. Each layer captures features or abstract representations of data extracted by the previous layer and learns to apply these features to a specific task. By combining multiple layers, deep learning models can recognize complex patterns and relationships in data that would be challenging to capture with traditional algorithms.

One fascinating aspect of deep learning is its ability to automatically extract features from the data, without relying on manually defined features. This approach allows models to develop a deeper understanding of the data and recognize complex features that may be difficult for humans to grasp.

For example, a deep learning model analyzing images can automatically learn edges, textures, shapes, and even abstract concepts like faces or objects without explicitly defining these features beforehand.

Another exciting aspect of deep learning is its capacity to process large amounts of data. The more data available to the model, the better it can learn patterns and relationships. This has led to significant improvements in performance in many application areas. In image recognition, for instance, deep learning models can accurately identify and classify objects in images. In natural language processing, deep learning enables automatic translation of texts or generating natural language text.

The training phase of deep learning models is often time-consuming and computationally intensive due to the depth and complexity of the models. It requires powerful hardware, such as graphics processing units (GPUs) or specialized application-specific integrated circuits (ASICs), to perform calculations efficiently.

Thanks to continuous advancements in hardware technology, these resources are becoming increasingly accessible, allowing researchers and developers to apply deep learning in a wider range of applications.

An exciting development in the field of deep learning is the use of generative models. These models can generate new data that is similar to the trained data. By employing generative models, realistic images can be created, indistinguishable from real photos, for example. This has applications in areas such as creative design, the entertainment industry, and virtual reality, opening up new possibilities for content generation and enabling artists and designers to unleash their creativity.

Despite the impressive progress and versatility of deep learning, there are challenges that need to be considered. One of them is the need for large amounts of data to train accurate models. However, in some application areas, only limited data may be available, which can restrict the effectiveness of deep learning models. As a result, researchers are actively working on methods to enhance machine learning with limited data to overcome this obstacle.

Another topic of concern is the explainability of deep learning models. Often, it's difficult to understand why a model made a specific decision. This "black box" problem can raise concerns in sensitive areas such as medical diagnostics, where doctors and experts may not be able to comprehend how a model arrived at its decision. Developing methods for explainability of deep learning models is an active research area to ensure trust and transparency in decision-making.

Overall, deep learning is an exciting and rapidly advancing technology with tremendous potential. It has allowed us to gain even deeper insights into complex data and make more precise predictions. With ongoing research and development, we will undoubtedly discover further exciting applications of deep learning.

It will be fascinating to see how this technology shapes our future and opens up new possibilities in various domains. The combination of deep analysis, automatic feature extraction, and powerful data processing makes deep learning a powerful tool for artificial intelligence, offering exciting prospects for innovative solutions in the modern world.

Chapter 8: Natural Language Processing

In this chapter, we dive into natural language processing (NLP), an intriguing field of artificial intelligence that deals with processing and analyzing human language. Natural language is incredibly complex and nuanced, which makes developing techniques to process and interpret it a big challenge. NLP enables computers to understand, analyze, and even interact with human language.

A fundamental concept in NLP is breaking down texts into smaller units called tokens. These tokens can be words, sentences, or even individual characters. By breaking down texts into tokens, algorithms can access specific features and recognize patterns in language. This is an important first step in natural language processing.

One of the fundamental tasks in NLP is text classification. It involves categorizing a given text into predefined categories or classes. This can include tasks like classifying emails as spam or non-spam, detecting sentiments in texts, or identifying topics in news articles. By using machine learning algorithms, especially supervised learning, models can be trained to automatically classify texts.

Another important concept in natural language processing is named entity recognition. It aims to identify and extract relevant information such as names, locations, organizations, or time expressions in a text.

Named entity recognition is a crucial component of information extraction, allowing structured information to be extracted from unstructured texts. This is particularly useful in processing large amounts of text data, such as analyzing customer feedback or extracting information from news articles.

A significant advancement in natural language processing is automatic machine translation. With the help of machine learning algorithms, especially neural machine learning, computer programs can be developed to automatically translate texts from one natural language to another.

This has led to impressive results and greatly facilitated communication between different language groups. Modern translation systems like Google Translate are built on these techniques and are continuously being improved to enhance translation quality.

Another exciting application of natural language processing is language generation. It involves computer programs generating texts or dialogues in natural language. This is used, for example, in chatbots or virtual assistants to enable human-like conversations.

By using machine learning techniques, particularly recurrent neural networks, models can be developed to generate meaningful and coherent texts based on inputs or contexts.

Another significant challenge in natural language processing is semantic analysis. It involves understanding and interpreting the meaning of sentences or texts. This is a complex task as the meaning of texts often depends on context, sentence structure, and understanding of underlying concepts.

Semantic analysis plays a vital role in searching for relevant information in large text collections, question-answering systems, or automatic text summarization.

With the advent of voice assistants like Siri, Alexa, and Google Assistant, natural language processing has gained even more importance. These voice assistants allow users to interact with their devices naturally using voice commands. The systems behind these voice assistants are based on techniques of speech recognition, natural language processing, and machine learning. They recognize and understand users' intents and perform corresponding actions.

Natural language processing has made tremendous progress and has already influenced many aspects of our daily lives. From automatic translations to voice assistants, it has revolutionized how we interact with technology. However, there are still many challenges to overcome, such as improving language understanding, addressing ambiguities and cultural differences, and ensuring privacy and security.

The future of natural language processing is promising. With further advancements in machine learning, neural networks, and the availability of large text datasets, systems will become even more powerful and accurate. We can look forward to exciting developments that will make natural language processing even more diverse and ubiquitous.

Chapter 9: Computer Vision

In this chapter, we're diving into a fascinating field of artificial intelligence called Computer Vision. It's all about teaching computers to process, analyze, and understand visual information. The goal is to enable computers to "see" and gain an understanding of visual data like images and videos.

Visual perception is a fundamental part of the human experience, and Computer Vision aims to transfer that ability to machines. This allows computers to comprehend visual information, recognize objects, identify patterns, and interpret complex scenes. Computer Vision finds wide applications in various fields like face recognition, autonomous driving, medical imaging, surveillance systems, and robotics.

A key concept in Computer Vision is feature extraction. It involves extracting relevant visual features from images or videos to make them accessible for further analysis and processing. These features can include edges, shapes, colors, or textures that capture information about the visual structure of objects or scenes. Techniques like the Canny edge detection algorithm or the Scale-Invariant Feature Transform (SIFT) are used to extract robust and discriminative features.

Object recognition is another exciting task in Computer Vision. It's about automatically identifying and classifying specific objects or categories of objects in images or videos. This can include recognizing faces, vehicles, or animals, for example. Object recognition often relies on machine learning and requires large amounts of annotated training data to train models that can reliably detect objects. Modern approaches like Convolutional Neural Networks (CNN) have made significant advancements in object recognition.

Another important concept in Computer Vision is image segmentation. It involves dividing an image into meaningful regions or segments to highlight specific objects or areas. This allows for a detailed analysis of images and a focus on relevant information. Methods like graph-based segmentation or semantic segmentation based on deep neural networks are used to achieve accurate and precise segmentations.

Spatial localization is yet another crucial aspect of Computer Vision. It aims to determine the precise position and orientation of objects in an image or a scene. This can be crucial for applications like augmented reality or navigation of autonomous vehicles. Techniques like Structure from Motion (SFM) or Simultaneous Localization and Mapping (SLAM) extract precise spatial information about the environment.

The development of Computer Vision systems has made significant progress, especially with the use of deep neural networks and machine learning. Modern systems can tackle complex visual tasks that were previously performed only by humans. However, there are still challenges in Computer Vision, such as the detection and classification of fine details, coping with lighting variations, or processing large amounts of visual data in real-time.

The future of Computer Vision is promising. With further advancements in machine learning, deep learning, and hardware technologies, computers will become increasingly powerful in processing and understanding visual information. Exciting developments can be expected in areas like autonomous vehicles, robotics, medicine, and augmented reality, where Computer Vision will play a crucial role. The ability of computers to interpret visual information will enhance our interaction with the digital world and open up new possibilities.

Let me share a personal anecdote about Computer Vision with you.

A few years ago, I had the pleasure of participating in an exciting research project that focused on the application of Computer Vision in archaeology. Our goal was to discover hidden patterns and structures on ancient artifacts using computer-based image analysis.

We closely collaborated with an archaeology team and gained access to a collection of ceramic vessels from a past civilization. Many of these vessels were damaged or covered in dirt and deposits, making it challenging to recognize their original form and decoration.

Using advanced Computer Vision algorithms and image processing techniques, we started analyzing the digitized images of the vessels. We developed specialized algorithms to identify and extract edges, patterns, and shapes in the images.

It was fascinating to witness how the computer gradually unveiled the hidden details of the vessels. We could recognize the original patterns and symbols that were concealed by time and the elements. By combining the results of our Computer Vision analysis with the knowledge of the archaeologists, we gained valuable insights into the culture and life of the ancient civilization.

One particular challenge was comparing the images captured from the vessels with reference images and databases to find similarities or connections to other archaeological findings. This is where machine learning came into play, analyzing the data, recognizing patterns, and drawing conclusions about the historical significance of the vessels.

Our work in archaeology using Computer Vision was an impressive example of how technology and science can go hand in hand. The ability to reveal hidden details and *patterns on ancient artifacts opens new avenues for research and our understanding of the past.*

This experience showed me how Computer Vision can make a significant contribution not only in modern applications like image recognition or autonomous driving but also in historical and cultural domains. The combination of technology and human knowledge can truly enable groundbreaking insights and discoveries.

Chapter 10: Artificial Intelligence in Medicine

Artificial intelligence (AI) has tremendous potential to revolutionize the diagnosis, treatment, and management of diseases in the field of medicine. There are various areas where AI is being employed to improve medical practices.

Diagnostic Support: AI can assist doctors in making diagnoses, particularly in analyzing medical images such as X-rays, CT scans, or MRI scans. By leveraging machine learning and specially designed algorithms, AI can identify patterns and anomalies that may be difficult for the human eye to detect. This enables faster and more accurate diagnosis of diseases, especially in complex cases.

Personalized Medicine: AI can contribute to developing personalized treatment plans. By analyzing genetic information, medical history, and other patient data, AI can make predictions about individual disease risks and suggest personalized treatment strategies. This allows for tailored patient care, where treatment is aligned with the specific needs and characteristics of each patient.

Drug Development: Developing new medications is a time-consuming and costly process. AI can help accelerate this process by analyzing large amounts of data and identifying patterns in drug research. By predicting the effects of compounds on specific diseases, AI can aid in identifying promising candidates for drug development. This can lead to more efficient research processes and the development of more effective medications.

Patient Monitoring: Through the use of wearable devices and sensors, AI can continuously collect and analyze health data. This enables real-time monitoring of patients' health conditions. Deviations from normal patterns can be detected, and early warnings can be provided for potential issues. This allows for timely intervention and can help prevent serious health complications.

Robot-Assisted Surgery: AI is increasingly being employed in robot-assisted surgery. By precisely controlling robots, surgeons can perform minimally invasive procedures. The robots work under the guidance of doctors and can execute highly precise movements. This results in reduced risks, faster recovery times, and better outcomes for patients.

However, integrating AI into medical practice is not without challenges. Data privacy, ethical considerations, and the need for careful validation of developed algorithms are important aspects that must be taken into account. Ensuring the security of patient data and maintaining confidentiality are of utmost importance.

Despite these challenges, applying AI in medicine offers significant benefits. It can assist doctors in diagnosis, develop personalized treatment strategies, accelerate drug development, improve patient monitoring, and advance surgical practices. It is an exciting time where technology and medical expertise come together to enhance healthcare and promote human well-being.

How I became interested in artificial intelligence?

It was a sad time in my life when I experienced the loss of a loved one due to the lack of artificial intelligence in medical diagnosis. My grandmother, who had been experiencing health problems for some time, had been to the hospital several times to have her symptoms evaluated. The doctors were striving to make an accurate diagnosis, but it was challenging as her symptoms were diverse and difficult to interpret.

The doctors conducted various tests and utilized their extensive experience to find a possible cause for her complaints. Unfortunately, this process took several weeks, and multiple opinions from different doctors were required. In the meantime, my grandmother's health continued to decline, and she grew weaker.

It was at this time that I first heard about the advancements in artificial intelligence in medical diagnosis. I read about the possibilities of AI-based systems being able to analyze large amounts of medical data and identify patterns that may not be immediately recognizable to human doctors. I wondered if this could have helped my grandmother.

Unfortunately, the assistance of artificial intelligence came too late for my grandmother. She eventually received a diagnosis, but it was too late to initiate an effective treatment. Her health continued to deteriorate, and she eventually passed away.

This experience made me reflect and contemplate the significance of artificial intelligence in medical practice. If there had been a system back then that analyzed my grandmother's symptoms and assisted the doctors in making a diagnosis, who knows if she would have had a better chance of survival.

I am convinced that integrating artificial intelligence into medical diagnostics has the potential to save lives and improve diagnostic accuracy. It is a way to combine human expertise with machine intelligence to achieve more efficient and precise results.

My hope is that in the future, artificial intelligence will become widely available and accessible in medical practice, aiding doctors in making faster and more accurate diagnoses. No one should have to suffer the loss of a loved one because a disease went undetected in time. The integration of artificial intelligence can help bridge this gap and elevate patient care to a new level.

Chapter 11: Autonomous Systems

Autonomous systems are a fascinating branch of artificial intelligence (AI) that has the ability to perform complex tasks independently, without human intervention or instructions. These systems rely on advanced algorithms, machine learning, and sensor technologies that enable them to perceive their environment, make decisions, and take actions.

A prominent example of autonomous systems is autonomous driving. Self-driving cars are equipped with a variety of sensors such as cameras, radar, and lidar to perceive their surroundings and collect real-time data. Using algorithms and machine learning, they analyze this data to recognize the road, traffic signs, other vehicles, and pedestrians.

Based on this information, they can make decisions such as adjusting speed, changing lanes, or braking to avoid collisions. The use of autonomous vehicles has the potential to improve road safety, make traffic flow more efficiently, and reduce accidents.

In robotics, autonomous systems are used to enable robots to independently perform complex tasks. These robots can perceive their environment, navigate around obstacles, grasp objects, and carry out various actions. An example is industrial robotics, where robots are used in the manufacturing industry to efficiently perform repetitive tasks. By employing autonomous robots, productivity can be increased, and the accuracy of production processes can be improved.

Moreover, autonomous robots can also be deployed in hazardous environments such as disaster areas or space exploration to reduce risks to human lives.

Drones are another example of autonomous systems. They can be used in various fields such as aerial photography, infrastructure inspection, agricultural monitoring, and deliveries. Autonomous drones are capable of flying pre-programmed routes and using various sensors to perceive their environment. They can recognize objects, perform measurements, capture images and videos, or even deliver small packages. The use of autonomous drones can lead to more efficient and cost-effective solutions for various applications.

Autonomous systems also play an increasingly important role in the logistics industry. They can be used to optimize supply chains, manage inventory, and perform automated sorting and packaging processes. Autonomous systems enable more efficient distribution of goods, minimize delays and errors, and contribute to cost savings. For example, autonomous robots can be deployed in warehouses to identify, track, and sort goods, significantly enhancing logistics efficiency.

Despite the many benefits autonomous systems offer, there are also challenges that need to be addressed. Safety is of paramount importance, especially in the case of autonomous vehicles where human lives are at stake. It is crucial for autonomous systems to have robust algorithms and safeguards to avoid unwanted events and address potential security vulnerabilities. Additionally, legal and ethical questions regarding the responsibility and liability of autonomous systems need to be clarified.

However, autonomous systems are undoubtedly an exciting field of research that has the potential to transform our daily lives and revolutionize many sectors. Through further advancements and deployment of autonomous systems, we will experience new opportunities for efficiency improvement, enhanced safety, and task automation. It remains intriguing to observe how this technology will continue to evolve and the impact it will have on our society.

To further enhance autonomous systems, various approaches can be pursued. Here are two ways in which these systems can be optimized

Advancement of algorithms and machine learning:
Through continuous research and development of new algorithms and machine learning techniques, autonomous systems can improve their capabilities. This includes the development of more advanced methods for processing and interpreting sensor information, decision-making, and learning from experience. New approaches like deep learning enable autonomous systems to recognize even more complex patterns and make better decisions. Improving algorithms and machine learning can enhance the performance and reliability of autonomous systems.

Sensor and data improvements:
The quality and accuracy of sensors used in autonomous systems play a crucial role in their performance. Advancements in sensor technologies enable autonomous systems to capture more precise and comprehensive information about their environment. Improved cameras, lidar systems, radar sensors, and other sensors allow autonomous systems to perceive the environment in more detail and with greater reliability. Furthermore, the availability and quality of training data are of great importance. Access to larger and more diverse datasets enables autonomous

systems to be better prepared for various situations and scenarios, enhancing their decision-making ability and ability to tackle complex challenges.

By combining these approaches - advancing algorithms and machine learning, as well as improving sensors and data - autonomous systems can be further enhanced in their performance and reliability. This will help expand their application areas and create new possibilities in various industries, from transportation and robotics to logistics and beyond.

Chapter 12: Ethics and Artificial Intelligence

Ethics in relation to artificial intelligence (AI) is a super complex topic that raises many ethical questions. With the increasing prevalence of AI technologies, it is crucial to understand and consider the moral and societal implications of these technologies. In the following, I will explain some of the key ethical aspects related to AI in detail.

One central ethical aspect is the transparency of AI systems. It is important to understand how decisions are made by AI systems and what factors come into play. Transparency allows people to comprehend the logic and basis behind the decisions and, if necessary, verify them. This is particularly important when AI systems are deployed in areas that have significant impacts on the lives and well-being of people, such as healthcare or judiciary.

Another important ethical aspect is the accountability of AI systems. Clear responsibilities need to be established to ensure that errors or biases can be recognized and corrected. If, for example, AI systems make faulty or discriminatory decisions, mechanisms must be in place to rectify them and hold the responsible parties accountable. Accountability for the decisions made by AI systems is crucial to maintain people's trust in these technologies.

Fairness of AI systems is another ethical aspect. AI algorithms and models should be developed in a way that does not support discrimination based on gender, race, religion, or other personal characteristics. It is of utmost importance to ensure that AI systems act fairly and treat people equally, regardless of their individual attributes. This requires careful selection and verification of training data to ensure it is representative and free from biases.

The protection of privacy and data security is another ethical aspect that needs to be considered in the development and application of AI systems. AI systems often process large amounts of data, including personal and sensitive information. It is of utmost importance to take appropriate security measures to prevent misuse or unauthorized access to this data. Privacy regulations and policies should be followed to ensure that people's privacy is preserved, and their personal information is protected.

The impact of AI on jobs and the workforce is also an ethically relevant question. The use of AI technologies can lead to automation and increased efficiency, potentially endangering jobs. It is important to take appropriate measures to mitigate the impact on workers. This can include retraining employees for new roles or creating new jobs related to AI technologies. It is important to ensure that the use of AI does not lead to social inequality or unemployment but rather creates opportunities for upskilling and new areas of work.

Another significant ethical aspect concerns the long-term consequences of AI on society as a whole. The deployment of AI technologies has the potential to fundamentally change our way of living and interacting. It is important to consider the impact of AI systems on various societal domains such as education, healthcare, transportation, or security. Comprehensive discussions about the use of AI in these areas are necessary to ensure that the technology is deployed for the benefit of society and in line with underlying ethical principles.

Lastly, the question of autonomy and responsibility of autonomous AI systems is an important ethical aspect. When AI systems can act autonomously and make decisions, clear rules and guidelines need to be established to ensure that their actions align with ethical principles. Developing mechanisms for monitoring and controlling autonomous AI systems is crucial to ensure that they act responsibly and do not make unwanted or dangerous decisions.

The ethical issues related to artificial intelligence require ongoing and comprehensive deliberation. It is important for technology companies, governments, scientists, and society as a whole to collaborate in developing and promoting ethical guidelines and principles. Only through responsible and ethically grounded development and application of AI can we ensure that this technology is used for the benefit of all people and in line with our moral and societal values.

Problems of AI with Ethics

Problems between artificial intelligence (AI) and ethics can arise in various areas. One central problem is the potential bias and discrimination that can occur in AI systems. This happens when algorithms make faulty or discriminatory decisions due to uneven training data or biases. An example of this is an AI system that analyzes job applications and makes unfair selection decisions based on gender or race. This poses an ethical challenge as it can lead to unequal treatment and discrimination.

Another problem is the transparency of AI systems. Often, the decision-making processes of AI systems are complex and difficult for humans to understand. This can result in a loss of trust, as people do not comprehend how decisions are made and what factors come into play. Particularly in areas such as healthcare or judiciary, where AI systems can have significant impacts, ensuring transparency is crucial to ensure accountability and trust in the technology.

The protection of privacy and data security is another ethical aspect that must be considered in the development and application of AI systems. AI systems often process large amounts of data, including personal and sensitive information. It is of utmost importance to take appropriate security measures to prevent misuse or unauthorized access to this data. Privacy regulations and policies should be followed to ensure that people's privacy is preserved, and their personal information is protected.

Another ethical problem concerns the accountability of AI systems. If AI systems can act autonomously and make decisions, clear rules and guidelines need to be established to ensure that their actions align with ethical principles. For example, when an autonomous vehicle encounters a potentially dangerous situation, the question arises of who is responsible for the decisions made by the vehicle.

It is important to develop mechanisms for monitoring and controlling autonomous AI systems to ensure that they act responsibly and do not make unwanted or dangerous decisions.

These examples shows the complex ethical challenges in dealing with artificial intelligence. It is crucial to acknowledge these problems and develop solutions to ensure that AI technologies are used responsibly and in line with our ethical values. This requires close collaboration between technology companies, governments, scientists, and society as a whole to develop and promote ethical guidelines that safeguard human rights, fairness, and societal benefits.

Chapter 13: Artificial Intelligence in Business

Artificial intelligence (AI) has had a significant impact on the business world in recent years. In the age of digitalization and technological advancement, AI opens up numerous opportunities to help companies operate more efficiently, make better decisions, and develop innovative products and services.

One important application of AI in business is process automation. By employing AI systems, repetitive and time-consuming tasks can be automated, leading to a significant increase in efficiency. Routine tasks such as data analysis, customer communication, or accounting can be taken over by AI systems, allowing employees to focus on more challenging and strategic tasks. This optimizes resource utilization and enhances a company's productivity.

Another critical area where AI is applied in business is data analysis. Companies possess vast amounts of data, and AI systems can help extract valuable insights and patterns from this data. By using machine learning algorithms, AI systems can analyze complex data, identify trends, and make precise predictions. This enables companies to make informed decisions, improve their marketing strategies, better understand customer needs, and offer personalized offerings.

Furthermore, AI enables the development of innovative products and services. By employing AI technologies, companies can explore new business models and differentiate themselves from competitors. For example, personalized recommendation systems based on AI algorithms can provide customers with tailored suggestions, or virtual assistants can enhance customer service. Such innovations not only contribute to customer satisfaction but can also lead to increased revenue and strengthen a company's competitiveness.

Another example of AI in business is the application of machine learning in finance. AI systems can analyze large volumes of financial data and identify patterns that may elude human analysts. This enables more accurate risk assessment, more efficient portfolio management, and early detection of fraudulent activities. As a result, financial companies can make informed decisions and optimize their business processes.

However, it is important to note that the use of AI in business also brings challenges. Privacy and security, for instance, are crucial aspects to consider when implementing AI systems. Responsible handling of sensitive corporate and customer data is of utmost importance to prevent data breaches and maintain customer trust.

Overall, the use of AI in business presents tremendous potential for transforming companies and developing innovative solutions. It offers opportunities for efficiency gains, data-driven decision-making, and creating differentiated competitive advantages. Through careful planning, implementation, and monitoring, companies can harness the benefits of AI while ensuring adherence to ethical standards and fulfilling social responsibilities.

The use of artificial intelligence in business offers exciting possibilities and has become a significant driver of innovation, efficiency improvement, and competitive advantages. Companies across industries are increasingly recognizing the value and potential of AI technologies to optimize their business processes and explore new avenues.

In the next chapter, we will explore another fascinating application of artificial intelligence: AI in research. Here, we will delve into how AI technologies assist researchers and scientists in solving complex problems, gaining new insights, and making groundbreaking discoveries. The combination of AI and research has the potential to accelerate progress in various scientific disciplines and expand the horizons of human knowledge.

So let's dive into the captivating world of AI in research and discover how these technologies contribute to gaining new scientific knowledge and pushing the boundaries of what is possible.

Chapter 14: Artificial Intelligence in Research

In today's world, artificial intelligence (AI) also has a significant impact on research. The combination of human intelligence and machine power opens up entirely new possibilities for addressing complex scientific challenges, analyzing data, and making groundbreaking discoveries.

One area where AI plays a big role in research is data analysis. Researchers often face the challenge of processing large amounts of data and extracting valuable information from it. This is where AI algorithms come into play, capable of recognizing patterns and correlations in the data, developing complex models, and making precise predictions. This AI-powered data analysis enables researchers to gain new insights, test hypotheses, and validate scientific theories.

An important aspect of AI in research is its support in the discovery of new drugs and treatment methods. The search for new medications often requires years of research and complex analyses. AI can help expedite this process by searching large databases, identifying patterns in existing drugs, and suggesting new drug candidates. This enables researchers to pursue more targeted and efficient approaches to drug development and potentially discover life-saving therapies.

Furthermore, AI plays a crucial role in robotics and laboratory automation. Robots, with the help of AI systems, can take on tasks such as conducting experiments, preparing samples, and collecting data. This not only improves accuracy and efficiency but also expands the potential for new discoveries. AI-driven robots can perform complex experiments, analyze data in real-time, and assist researchers in gaining new insights.

Another field where AI is employed in research is the analysis of scientific texts and publications. With the help of AI systems, researchers can search through vast amounts of scientific literature, extract relevant information, and establish connections between different research works. This facilitates access to pertinent information and contributes to accelerating scientific progress.

However, it is important to emphasize that AI in research is not a substitute for human creativity and intuition. While AI systems can assist in data analysis and pattern recognition, the interpretation of results and formulation of new hypotheses ultimately remain the researchers' task. Close collaboration between humans and machines is crucial to fully harness the potential of AI in research.

Overall, the integration of artificial intelligence into research opens up a wide range of possibilities. It supports researchers in data analysis, drug development, laboratory automation, and scientific text analysis. By combining human creativity and machine power, AI in research can accelerate scientific progress, gain new insights, and push the boundaries of what is possible.

Chapter 15: Future Predictions and Challenges

The future of artificial intelligence (AI) holds both exciting opportunities and challenging aspects. In this chapter, we will explore the predictions for the future of AI and the associated challenges.

It is undeniable that AI will continue to play an increasingly significant role in the years to come. Many experts believe that AI technologies will be present in almost every aspect of life and business. From self-driving cars to intelligent assistants to personalized medicine, the applications of AI are diverse and open up new horizons.

One of the major challenges accompanying the advancement of AI is the question of ethics. How can we ensure that AI systems act ethically and respect our values and norms? Developing guidelines and standards for the responsible use of AI will be an important task to ensure that AI operates in line with our societal and moral principles.

Another central issue is the question of job transformation and displacement due to AI. It is undeniable that AI systems can replace human labor in many areas. This can lead to a reshaping of the job market and social challenges. Therefore, it is important to develop strategies to cope with the impact of AI on the job market, such as promoting lifelong learning and creating new job opportunities.

Another crucial aspect is the issue of data privacy. AI systems rely on large amounts of data and require access to personal information. It is crucial to ensure the protection of user privacy and the responsible use of data. Developing robust data protection policies and ensuring transparency and user control are of great importance.

In addition to these challenges, there are other aspects that will be relevant to the future of AI. These include issues of AI system security, responsibility in AI system decision-making, and the advancement of AI algorithms.

It is important that we are aware of these predictions and challenges and actively work on solutions. Collaboration among experts from various fields such as science, industry, and politics will be crucial to shaping the future of AI and ensuring its beneficial use for society.

Two possibilities in which artificial intelligence could develop:

Advancements in Generative AI:
Generative AI refers to systems that are capable of autonomously generating new content, whether it be in the form of texts, images, music, or even videos. While impressive results have already been achieved, there is still ample room for improvement. In the future, we could see more advanced generative AI models that can produce even more realistic and convincing content. This could lead to AI systems capable of composing complex literary works, creating high-quality artwork, or even generating realistic virtual worlds.

AI in Robotics:
Another exciting area of development is the integration of artificial intelligence into robotic systems. While robots are already being used in various fields, future AI-driven robots could possess advanced cognitive abilities. They could be capable of autonomously performing complex tasks, adapting to changing environments, and interacting with humans in a natural manner. For example, think of robot assistants in healthcare supporting elderly individuals or autonomous robots in agriculture that

can identify and treat plants selectively. By combining AI and robotics, we could witness a multitude of new applications that revolutionize our daily lives and various industries.

These examples are just a small selection of the many possibilities for the future development of artificial intelligence. It remains thrilling to observe how the technology evolves and what groundbreaking applications and innovations it brings forth.

Chapter 16: Artificial Intelligence in Pop Culture

The world of pop culture is a fascinating realm that constantly evolves and surprises us with new trends and ideas. Amidst this creative melting pot, artificial intelligence (AI) has found its rightful place. From movies to books, music, and video games, pop culture has embraced AI as a topic that fuels our imagination and makes us contemplate the boundaries of humanity.

In cinema, AI has taken over the silver screen, capturing our imagination with captivating stories. Films like "Blade Runner" and "Ex Machina" have transported us to a world where intelligent robots and artificial beings challenge our society. These movies not only depict a technological future but also prompt us to reflect on profound questions. What defines humanity? Can machines develop consciousness? How does the interaction between humans and machines influence our notions of identity and morality? AI in pop culture provides us with the opportunity to explore these questions and develop our own perspectives.

AI has also found its way into literature, giving rise to numerous masterpieces of science fiction. Authors like Isaac Asimov, Philip K. Dick, and William Gibson have created foundations for the genre of AI literature with works such as "I, Robot," "Do Androids Dream of Electric Sheep?," and "Neuromancer."

These books immerse us in fascinating worlds where AI systems have complex moral beliefs, struggle for autonomy, or even take control. They invite us to contemplate the impact of AI on our society and explore the limits of human imagination.

In addition to film and literature, AI has also reached the world of music. Artists like Kraftwerk, Daft Punk, and Radiohead have addressed themes of technology, robotics, and the relationship between humans and machines in their songs. Music becomes a medium that connects us with AI on an emotional level. It makes us reflect on the potential impact of AI on artistic production and encourages us to contemplate our own relationships with technology.

Video games also offer us the opportunity to interactively delve into the world of AI. Games like "Portal," "Deus Ex," and "Detroit: Become Human" present us with complex stories and decisions that influence the course of the narrative. These games confront us with moral dilemmas where we interact with AI characters and grapple with the ethical challenges of a technological future. They provide us with the opportunity to experience AI firsthand and make our own judgments and decisions.

AI in pop culture allows us to contemplate the possibilities and risks of artificial intelligence and reflect on our own fears and hopes. It serves as a source of inspiration but also as a warning about the consequences of thoughtless technological progress.

Through movies, books, music, and video games, pop culture opens up a space for us to explore the interactions between humans and machines and engage with the moral, ethical, and existential questions surrounding AI.

The world of artificial intelligence in pop culture is fascinating and diverse. It allows us to immerse ourselves in worlds where the boundaries between humans and machines blur and where we can explore the impact of AI on our society, identity, and future. Let us continue to enjoy the stories, movies, books, songs, and games that inspire us to contemplate the opportunities and challenges of artificial intelligence and gain new perspectives.

Chapter 17: Summary and Outlook

In this book, we've delved into the fascinating field of AI and explored various aspects and applications of this technology. Now, let's take a step back and look at the big picture to summarize the key insights.

In the first chapter, we examined the fundamentals of artificial intelligence. We learned that AI deals with the development of machines and systems capable of exhibiting human-like intelligence. We explored different types of AI, from weak AI that performs specific tasks to strong AI with general understanding and learning abilities.

In the chapter on "Machine Learning," we focused on one of the key technologies of artificial intelligence. Machine learning enables computers to learn from data and recognize patterns without being explicitly programmed. We explored various types of machine learning, such as supervised and unsupervised learning, and their applications in areas like image recognition, language processing, and predictive analytics.

The chapter on "Neural Networks" provided us with a deeper insight into a specific form of machine learning. Neural networks are inspired by the functioning of the human brain and consist of artificial neurons connected to each other. We saw that neural networks can recognize complex patterns and tackle tasks like face recognition, language translation, and decision-making.

In the "Deep Learning" chapter, we looked at an advancement in machine learning. Deep learning utilizes deep neural networks with many layers to handle even more complex tasks. We witnessed impressive progress in deep learning, particularly in image and speech recognition, as well as autonomous vehicle technology.

The application of artificial intelligence in various fields was explored in chapters on AI in business, medicine, research, and pop culture. We shed light on the benefits and challenges of integrating AI into these domains and saw how AI drives innovation, optimizes processes, and creates new possibilities.

Lastly, it is crucial to consider the ethical implications of artificial intelligence. In the chapter on "Ethics and Artificial Intelligence," we discussed topics such as data privacy, transparency, fairness, and responsibility. It is essential that we develop and deploy AI responsibly to ensure it contributes to the well-being of society.

The outlook for the future of artificial intelligence is filled with potential and challenges. We can expect AI to permeate more areas of our lives and open up new opportunities. At the same time, we must grapple with the ethical, social, and legal questions associated with the further development of AI.

Overall, in this book, we've gained a comprehensive understanding of the fascinating field of artificial intelligence. From the basics to concrete applications, we've seen how AI is transforming our world and providing new perspectives. It is up to us to drive the advancement of artificial intelligence and use it for the betterment of humanity.

Conclusion

With this book on artificial intelligence, we embarked on an exciting journey into the world of intelligent machines. We learned the basics of AI, explored various techniques like machine learning and neural networks, and discovered the diverse applications of AI in fields such as business, medicine, research, and pop culture.

Artificial intelligence has the potential to fundamentally transform our world. It enables us to gain new insights, develop more efficient processes, and find innovative solutions to complex problems. At the same time, the advancements in AI also raise important ethical questions that we must not ignore. It is our responsibility to ensure that artificial intelligence is used for the benefit of society.

I hope this book has provided you with a comprehensive insight into the world of artificial intelligence. However, it is just the beginning. The journey into the fascinating world of technology has many more facets to offer. If you're interested in learning more about related topics, I invite you to explore the other books in the

"Simple Explanation" series. There, you will find more exciting subjects like robotics, virtual reality, blockchain, and much more.

Thank you for your attention, and I hope you have benefited from this book. Artificial intelligence will undoubtedly play an increasingly significant role in our lives. Let us continue to delve into the world of technology with curiosity and responsibility, exploring the opportunities and challenges of artificial intelligence together.

Wishing you all the best on your further exploration journey!

Kevin van Olafson